The Ultimate Puzzle Book

Visual Exercises
Math Problems
Brain Teasers
Logic Puzzles
Word Games
Mazes

*

J.J. Wiggins

ISBN: 978-1539149026
Edition: 1.4

"A puzzle a day keeps the doctor away."
— Unknown

Contents

Mazes 1

Teleporters ***** 1

Lights Out ***** 2

Bombs Away ***** 3

Computer Chip ***** 4

Out Of Control ***** 5

Seeing Circles ***** 6

Dizzy Dizzy ***** 7

Teleporters Galore ***** 8

Narrow Escape ***** 9

Deadly Fall ***** 10

Funky Clouds ***** 11

Lights Out 2 ***** 12

Out Of Control 2 ***** 13

Triangles of Doom ***** 14

Cup And Medal ***** 15

Word Games 17

Word Square ***** 17

Secret Animals ***** 18

Easy Crossword ***** 19

Two Blanks ***** 20

Animal Search ***** 21

Secret Riddle ** **** 22

Word Square 2 *** ** 23

Missing Vowels ** *** 24

Missing Consonants *** ** 24

School Subjects *** ** 25

Animated Films *** ** 26

Three Blanks *** ** 27

Hard Crossword **** * 28

Unscramble Me *** ** 29

Sally's Secret Job ***** 30

Visual Challenges 31

Full Circles * **** 31

Two Shapes * **** 32

X's And O's * **** 33

Mystery Cube ** *** 34

Broken Clock *** ** 35

Mixed Messages ** *** 36

Scrambled * **** 37

True Symmetry ** *** 38

Hidden Words *** ** 39

Tricky Triangles *** ** 40

Three Shapes ** *** 41

Shifty Symbols *** ** 42

Mystery Cube 2 ***** 43

Scrambled 2 *** ** 44

Hidden Words 2 **** * 45

Math Problems 47

Addition ** *** 47

New Time ** *** 48

Word Seesaw ** *** 49

Adding Pets *** ** 50

Subtraction ** *** 51

Big Cube ** *** 52

Triangle Sum *** ** 53

This And That ** *** 54

Multiplication *** ** 55

Word Seesaw 2 *** ** 56

Adding Directions ***** 57

Division *** ** 58

Missing Cubes **** * 59

What It Takes *** ** 60

Star Sum **** * 61

Visual Puzzles 63

Numbers Connect * **** 63

Continuous Lines ** *** 64

Falling Tiles ** *** 65

Cut The Shapes ** *** 66

Tricky Sticks ** *** 67

Puzzle Pieces * **** 68

Picture Grid ** *** 69

Cooking Show ** *** 70

Numbers Connect 2 *** ** 71

Continuous Lines 2 **** 72

Falling Tiles 2 **** 73

Stick Equations *** 74

Puzzle Pieces 2 *** 75

Fence Off ** 76

Picture Grid 2 *** 77

Logic Puzzles 79

Odd One Out * 79

Random Letters ** 79

Bomb Report ** 80

Johnny's Secret *** 81

Letters In A Square * 82

Sudoku ** 83

Sally's Picnic ** 84

Three Honest Kids ** 84

Shape Riddles *** 85

Big Family ** 86

Count The Months ** 87

Math Maze *** 88

Bomb Report 2 **** 89

Sally's Secret ***** 90

Sudoku 2 **** 91

Brain Teasers 93

The Butterfly ** 93

The Purple Friend * 93

River Crossing **** 94

Weird Thanksgiving ** 94

Bless You * 94

The Cheater **** 95

Sally's Family * 95

Half A Cup ** 96

Two Coins * 96

Jack's Family ** 96

Matching Marbles ** 97

Ladder Escape **** 97

Gummi Bears * 98

The Butterfly 2 ***** 98

The Three Sisters **** 99

Answer Keys 101

Mazes 101

Word Games 106

Visual Challenges 109

Math Problems 114

Visual Puzzles 117

Logic Puzzles 122

Brain Teasers 126

– Mazes –

Teleporters ***** #1

Roboman must escape the clutches of the evil super villain, Elector! Get him to the exit by guiding him through the maze. Each symbol is a teleporter. Step on one to teleport to the matching symbol. Go!

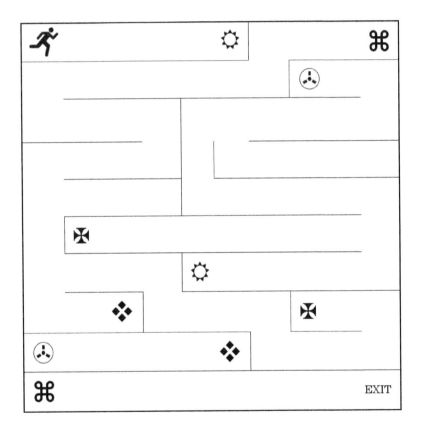

Lights Out ★★☆☆☆

Uh oh, Elector's henchmen have been alerted! Run, Roboman, run! The bad guys can spot him if he enters a room (white area) when the lights are still on. Help him escape by turning off the lights!

Rules: Roboman can't enter a room if the lights in that room are on, and, you're only allowed to turn off the lights in 7 rooms. Two of them have already been done for you.

Color 5 more rooms and lead Roboman to the exit.

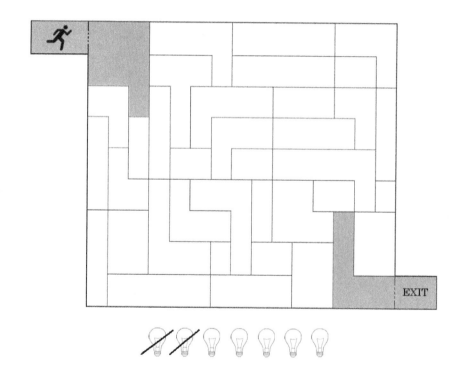

Mazes

Bombs Away **☆☆☆ #3

Things are about to get messy. Get Roboman to the exit before all the bombs explode. Don't touch any of them!

EXIT

Computer Chip *✳✳✳✳✳

Roboman's trapped in a computer chip! The snowflakes will lead him back to the real world. Get him to the exit before he's deleted!

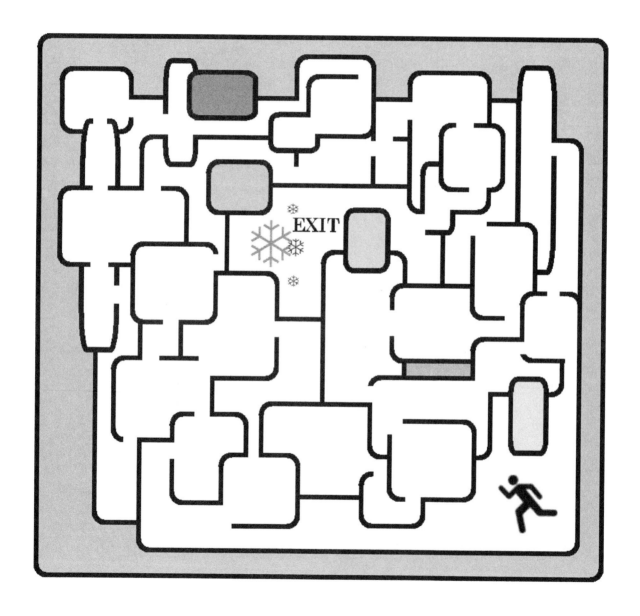

Mazes

Out Of Control **✱✱✱   #5

Be careful, the floors are slippery in this room! Once Roboman starts moving in one direction, he won't be able to stop.

Rules: In this slippery maze, Roboman must keep moving in one direction. When he hits an obstacle (a thick wall or a black square), he can turn to face left, right, up, or down, and then continue in the new direction.

Run, Roboman, run!

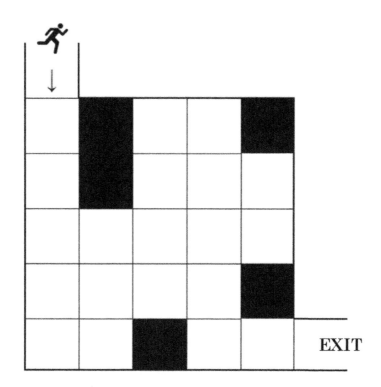

Seeing Circles ***✻✻ #6

So many circles! It's making Roboman see funny. Hopefully your vision is better. Get him to the exit.

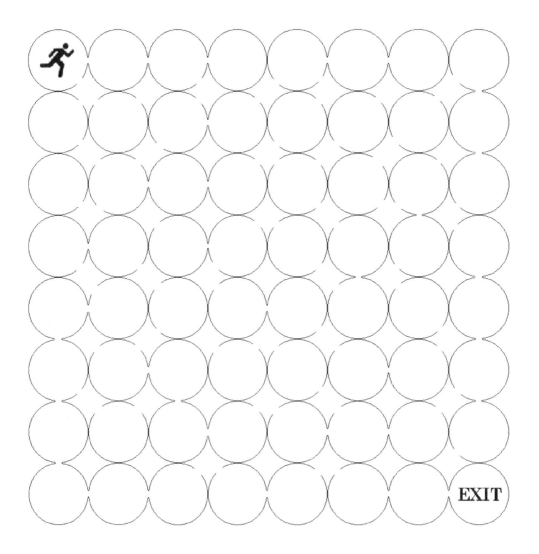

Bonus: How many *full* diamonds (the curvy shapes between four circles) are there in this maze? Color them in!

The walls are shaking! Roboman's getting super dizzy. Get him out of here before the whole place collapses.

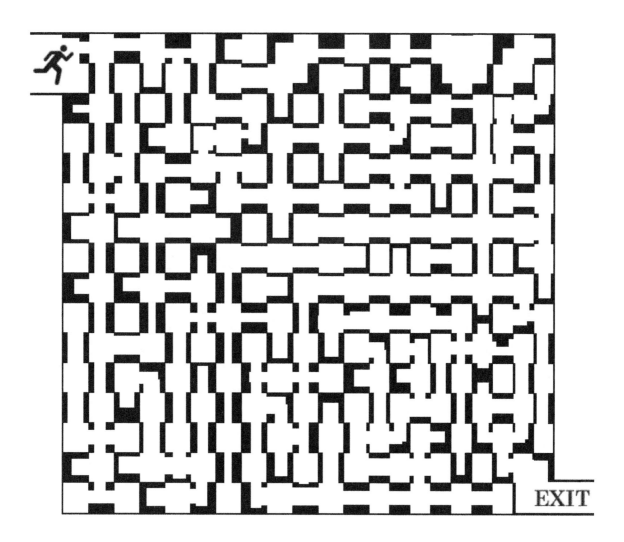

Teleporters Galore **✳✳✳ #8

What, more teleporters!? That darn Elector! Get Roboman to the exit before he's caught. Remember, step on one teleporter to warp to the matching one. Run!

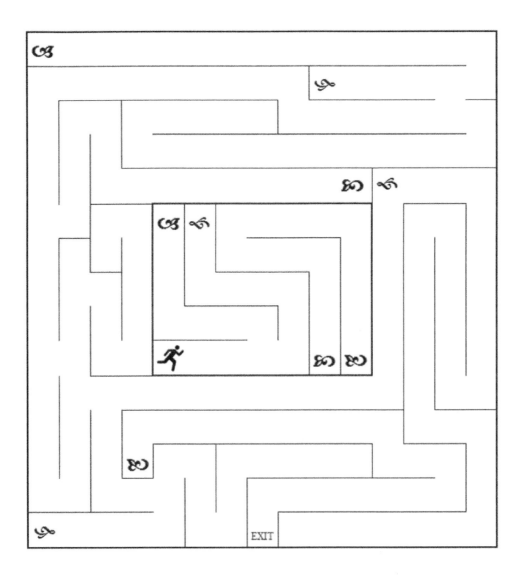

Roboman is close to escaping Elector's headquarters, but it only gets harder from here. Pay attention to the narrow passage ways or you might get lost. Get Roboman to the exit!

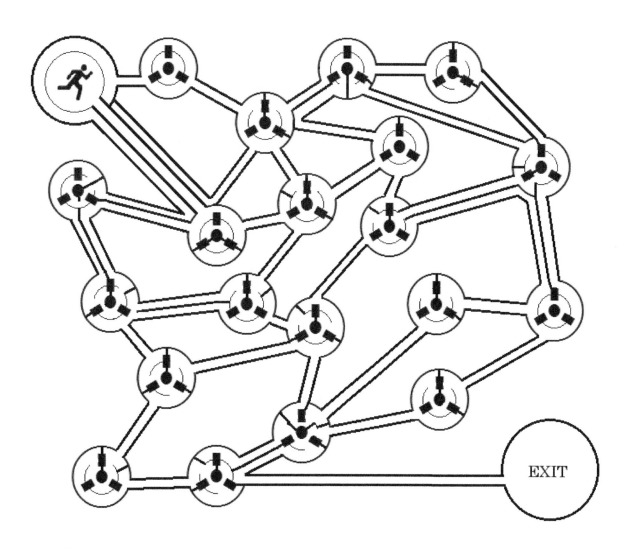

Deadly Fall **✳✳✳

Roboman is falling! Help him avoid the deadly spikes by coloring in the correct platforms (dotted lines). But don't block the path to the exit!

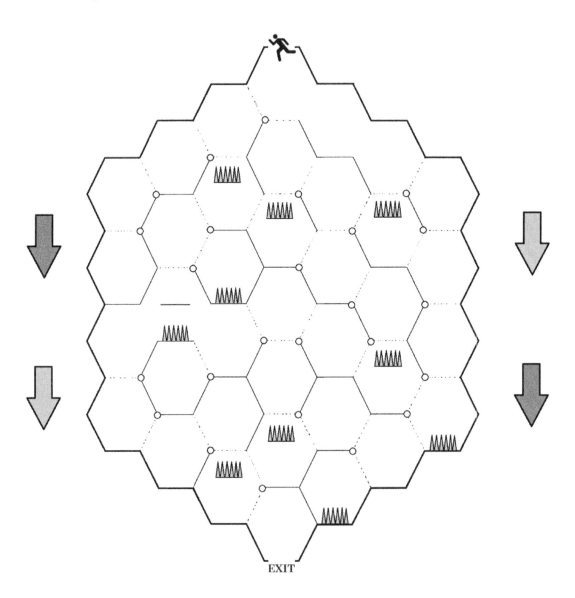

EXIT

Funky Clouds **✳✳✳ #11

Time to relax a bit in this maze filled with funky clouds.
Don't stay too long. Elector is still after Roboman. Guide our
hero to the exit!

EXIT

Lights Out 2 *****

Roboman has gotten himself in a pickle again! Help him escape by turning off the lights in the correct rooms. Remember, the bad guys can spot him if he enters a room (white area) when the lights are still on.

Rules: Roboman can't enter a room if the lights in that room are on, and, you are only allowed to turn off the lights in 10 rooms. Two of them have already been done for you!

Color 8 more rooms and lead Roboman to the exit.

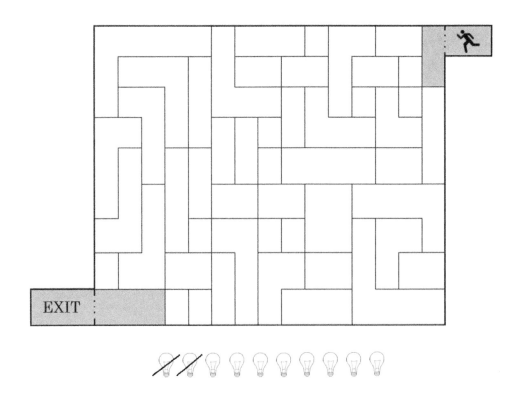

Out Of Control 2 ***** #13

Another room with slippery floors! Remember, once Roboman starts moving, he won't be able to stop.

Rules: Roboman must keep moving in one direction. When he hits an obstacle (a thick wall or a black square), he can turn to face left, right, up, or down, and then continue in the new direction.

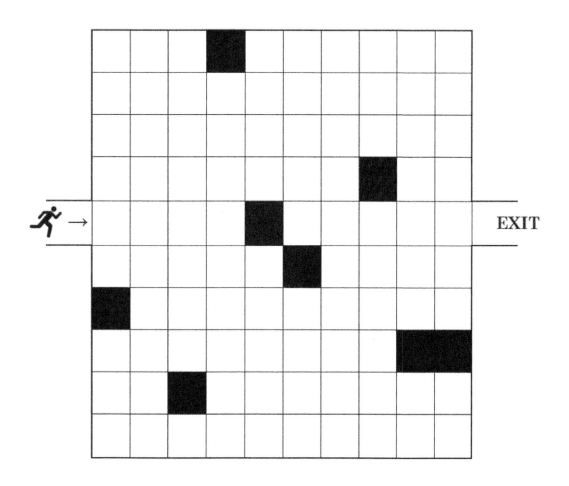

Triangles of Doom **✳✳✳ #14

The floors are going to collapse! Roboman must be very careful where he steps. Only the triangle-shaped tiles can support his weight. Guide him to the exit.

Rules: Roboman can't step on shapes with more than 3 sides, and, he can only step on a triangle that's touching the one he's on. Corners don't count!

To make it easier for you to see the path, color in the triangles.

This is the final maze in Elector's headquarters! Roboman must collect the trophy and the medal before heading for the exit. Good luck!

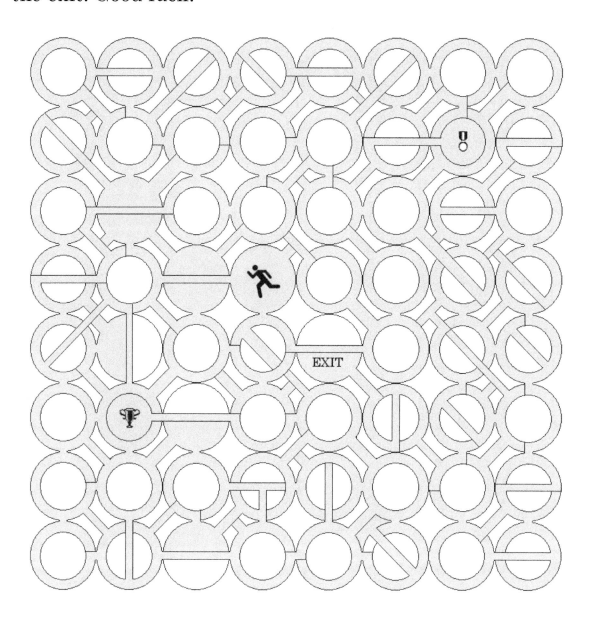

Mazes

Word Square ****** #16

Fill in the blank squares with any letter of the alphabet to make three-letter words. The numbers outside the square show you the direction of the word: either left to right or top to bottom. You can only put one letter in each blank square. And no making up words!

```
     4    5    6
   ┌────┬────┬────┐
 1 │    │ E  │ D  │
   ├────┼────┼────┤
 2 │ E  │    │ R  │
   ├────┼────┼────┤
 3 │ T  │ R  │    │
   └────┴────┴────┘
```

Write the words you create here:

1. _____   4. _____

2. _____   5. _____

3. _____   6. _____

Complete the word for an animal by filling in the blank(s).
They could be mammals, reptiles, insects, or amphibians.
Then, solve the riddle below with the letters in the circles!

1. (①__) E A R	11. __ A N __ A __ O (⑤__)
2. M __ N K __ __	12. __ S __ R I C __
3. O __ L	13. E __ G (⑥__) E
4. __ E B (②__) A	14. S E A (⑦__)
5. L __ (③__) N	15. (⑧__) G U A __ A
6. __ H A L __	16. __ I __ __ F F (⑨__)
7. __ U T T __ __ F __ __	17. R A __ C __ O __
8. P __ N G __ __ N	18. __ N __ K (⑩__)
9. (④__) H I P __ U N K	19. B __ A __ E R
10. __ E E __	20. R __ B __ I T

What do you call two dogs that are very good friends?

$\underline{\quad} \ \underline{\quad} \ \underline{\quad} - \underline{\quad} \ \underline{\quad} \ \underline{\quad} \ \underline{\quad} \ \underline{\quad} \ \underline{\quad} \ \underline{\quad}$
  1   2   3   4   5   6   7   8   9   10

Easy Crossword ******

Can you complete this easy crossword?

Across
1. A red fruit.
2. A sheet in a book.
3. An octopus has eight _____.
4. Wizards know how to use _____.
5. A dried grape.
6. Mom's husband.
7. An animal that looks like a horse.

Down
1. An animal that eats ants.
2. A type of bear.
3. Another word for test.
4. Cars need _____ to run.
5. Opposite of cry.
6. More than one mouse.
7. Sweet treats.

Complete the four-letter word by reading each clue and filling in the blanks.

1. very powerful individuals:

__ O D __

2. hands and feet are part of this:

__ O D __

3. a boy's name:

__ O D __

4. something you drink:

__ O D __

Animal Search **✳✳✳

How many animals can you find in the square below?
Forwards, backwards, up, down, and diagonals are all
allowed!

H	G	G	I	P
C	O	W	L	U
D	A	R	A	T
E	T	T	S	N
S	N	A	K	E

Write the words you find here:

1. _____   6. _____

2. _____   7. _____

3. _____   8. _____

4. _____   9. _____

5. _____

Why wasn't the turkey at Thanksgiving dinner? Solve the secret message to find out!

Rules: Each symbol represents a letter. Replace each symbol with the matching letter to reveal the answer to the riddle.

Hints:

♋ = A   ♎ = D   ✦ = E
♐ = F   ♓ = I   ● = L
◻ = R   ⤳ = S   ◆ = T
? = U   ◉ = W   ♉ = Y

Secret Message:

Word Square 2 *****

#22

Fill in the blank squares with any letter of the alphabet to make four letter words. The numbers show you the direction of the word: either left to right or top to bottom. You can only put one letter in each blank square. And no making up words!

```
        5   6   7   8
      ┌───┬───┬───┬───┐
  1   │ S │   │ A │ R │
      ├───┼───┼───┼───┤
  2   │   │ O │ L │   │
      ├───┼───┼───┼───┤
  3   │ O │ N │   │   │
      ├───┼───┼───┼───┤
  4   │ T │   │ S │   │
      └───┴───┴───┴───┘
```

Write the words you create here:

1. _____   5. _____

2. _____   6. _____

3. _____   7. _____

4. _____   8. _____

Missing Vowels **✸✸✸   #23

Sally sent a text message to her friend Rob and decided not to use any vowels. This is what she wrote:

Wht r y dng rght nw?

Can you figure out what she asked him?

Missing Consonants ***✸✸   #24

Rob got a message from his friend Sally and decided to play a trick on her. This is what he wrote back:

I' ai a oie.

Can you figure out his message? There is more than one answer! Be creative and see how many different sentences you can come up with!

Hint: It's a 4-word sentence.

Do you know your school subjects? There are 8 of them in this awesome grid of hexagons! Connect the letters to create a word. You can reuse letters for different words. We did one of them for you!

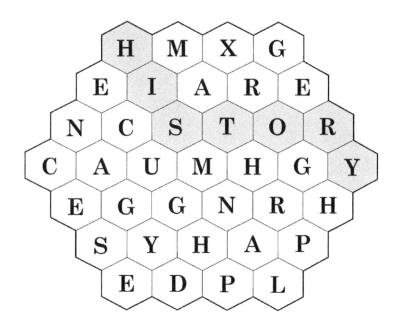

Write the words you find here:

1. H I S T O R Y   5. _____

2. _____   6. _____

3. _____   7. _____

4. _____   8. _____

Animated Films ***** #26

Complete the word for a movie by filling in the blank(s).
Then, solve the riddle below with the letters in the circles!

1. F R O (①) _ N
2. I _ E _ G E
3. _ _ R E K
4. _ I _ D I N _
   N E M (②)
5. W _ L L - _
6. P _ N (③) C _ H I O
7. T H _
   _ N C R E _ I _ L E _
8. _ L E E P _ N _
   B E _ U _ Y
9. _ P
10. _ E _ _ T Y _ N D
    _ H E _ E A _ T

11. M O _ S (④) E _ S I _ _ _
12. A _ A _ D I N
13. _ O Y _ T O _ Y
14. T _ E L I (⑤) _
    _ I N G
15. _ U N G _ U
    (⑥) A _ D A
16. _ _ R S
17. M A D _ _ _ _ _ C A R
18. _ A T A T O _ (⑦) L _ E
19. _ R _ C K - I _
    R A L _ _ _
20. _ O W _ O _ R A I _
    _ O U R _ R (⑧) G O N

Where's the favorite place for animals to be?

‾‾ ‾‾ ‾‾ ‾‾ ‾‾ ‾‾ ‾‾ ‾‾
1   2   3   4   5   6   7   8

Complete the six-letter word by reading each clue and filling in the blanks.

1. one of the four seasons:

__ __ R I N __

2. not very interesting:

__ __ R I N __

3. run really, really fast:

__ __ R I N __

4. a place where boats park:

__ __ R I N __

Can you complete this crossword? It won't be easy!

Across
1. December holiday.
2. Angry.
3. Creature.
4. Opposite of lose.
5. Paperwork.
6. Ready, set, ___!
7. Not off.
8. A boy's name.
9. Two divided by two.
10. US space agency.
11. You wear this with a suit.

Down
1. Outdoor activity.
2. A primary color.
3. There are sixty _____ in an hour.
4. For eating soup.
5. For eating pasta.
6. A very big house.
7. Guy who wears tights and a cape.
8. Not closed.
9. Not in.
10. A part of the body.

Unscramble each row of letters to uncover different fruits and vegetables. Once you're done, the answer to the riddle below will reveal itself in the dark squares!

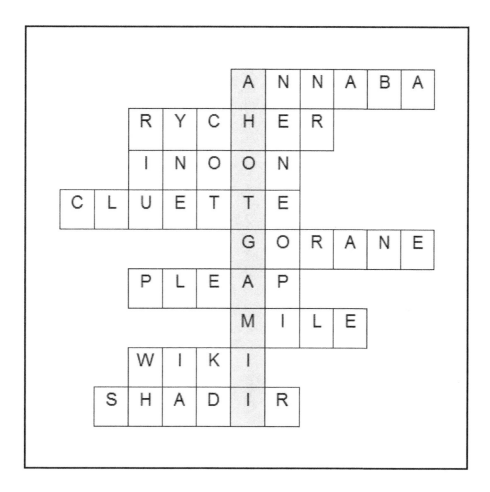

What do you call two vegetables that are very good friends?

___ ___ ___ - ___ ___ ___ ___ ___ ___
1   2   3   4   5   6   7   8   9

Sally's Secret Job ***** #30

Sally got a summer job, but she doesn't want to tell her friend John what it is. Instead, she gives him a secret message. Help John figure it out!

Hints:

ᏸᏬ = A		Ᏺ = E or O	
Ꮭ = Y		Ꮄ = E or O	
ᏸᏬ = H		✦ = T or S	
Ꮼ = L		Ᏺ = T or S	
● = R		Ⅹ = B or M	

Secret Message:

ᏲᏬᏸᏬᏄ ᏲᏄᏬᏬᏲ
ᏲᏄᏸᏲᏸᏄᏬᏬᏲ
ᏜᏭ ✦ᏸᏬᏄ
ᏲᏄᏸ ᏲᏸᏲ●Ꮄ.

Full Circles ****** #31

How many *full* circles are there in the picture below? Color them in!

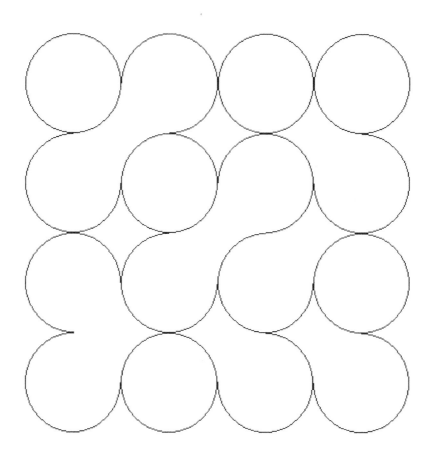

Two Shapes *✱✱✱✱✱   #32

Each picture is created using 2 shapes. Can you figure out what they are? Write the names of the shapes in the space provided.

1.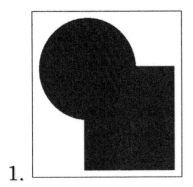

2.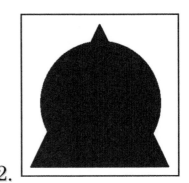

3.

4.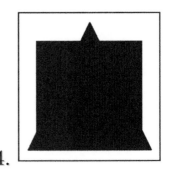

X's And O's *✱✱✱✱

X's and O's are moving on a 4x4 grid! In the first picture (left), the O is in the top right corner, and the X is in the bottom left corner. Study the next two pictures (middle and right). Do you see a pattern? Circle the correct answer.

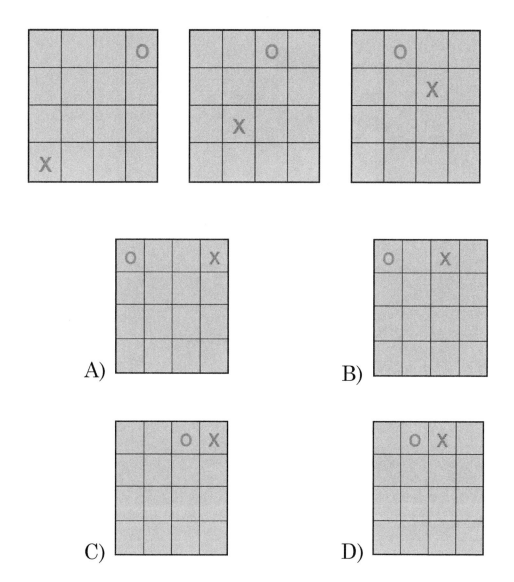

A)

B)

C)

D)

This big cube has 6 faces, and each face has a different symbol. Which of the images (A, B, C, D) can be created by unfolding the cube? There may be more than one right answer! Circle the correct ones.

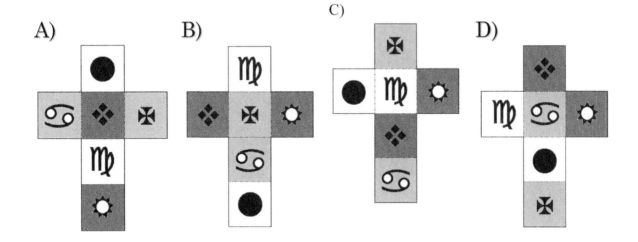

A)

B)

C)

D)

Johnny wakes up from bed and looks at his alarm clock. It reads:

A bit later, he looks at it again, and it reads:

A minute later, he looks at it yet again, and it reads:

He thinks the alarm clock is broken. What do you think? What time should it read next?

A)    B)    C)    D)

Let's test your brain! Can you read the following messages made of letters and numbers? Write the answers down and check later.

Message #1:
7H15 M3554G3 W1LL 53LF D3S7RUC7
1N F1V3 M1NU735!

Message #2:
73N, N1N3, 31GH7, 53V3N, 51X,
F1V3, F0UR, 7HR33, 7W0, 0N3,
K4B00M!

Message #3:
0NC3 UP0N 4 71M3, 7H3R3 W45 4 L177L3 B0Y
N4M3D 4LB3R7 WH0 W4N73D 70 347 C4K3 4LL D4Y.
7H3 3ND!

Message #4:
R0535 4R3 R3D, V10L375 4R3 BLU3
PUZZL35 4R3 51LLY, 4ND 50 4R3 Y0U!

The pictures below have been cut up into different parts. Can you figure out what they are? Rearrange the pieces and draw the picture. Then, write down the name of the thing found in the picture.

1.

2.

3.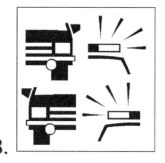

4.

True Symmetry ****** #38

Which of the 4 pictures below is symmetrical and which is not? Circle the picture(s) that are not symmetrical.

Hint: "Symmetrical" means that you can cut the picture in half and each half will look like a reflection of the other.

A)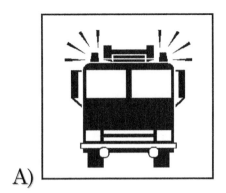

B)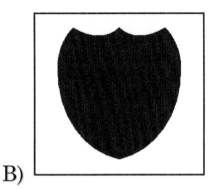

C)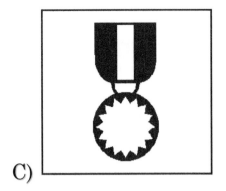

D)

There are 3 words hidden behind the black shapes. Can you see them?

Hint: Draw lines around the black shapes to help you see better!

How many different triangles can you find in the picture below?

Hint: There are triangles of different sizes in the picture.

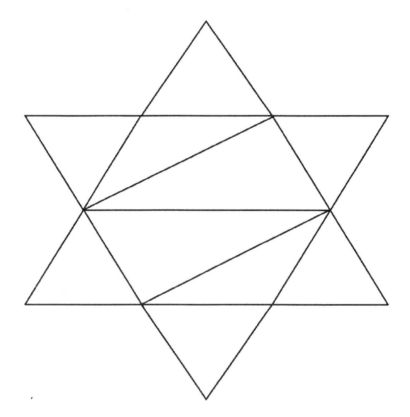

Three Shapes **✻✻✻

Each picture is created using 3 shapes. Can you figure out what they are? Write the names of the shapes in the space provided.

1.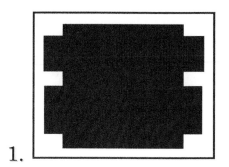

2.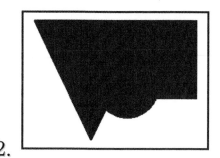

3.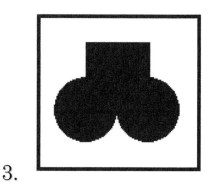

4.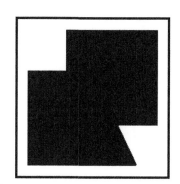

Symbols are moving in every direction on a 5x5 grid! Can you figure out their pattern? Circle the correct answer.

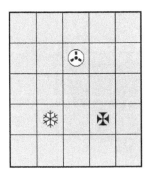 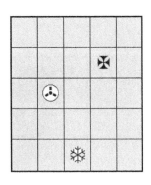 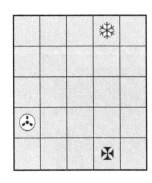

?

A) 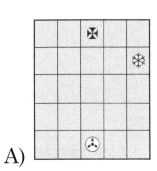 B)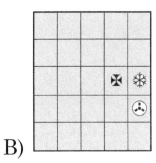

C) 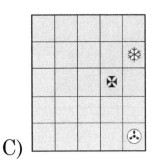 D)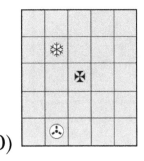

Mystery Cube 2 *****

You cut a piece of paper and draw a different symbol on each of the 6 squares. Which cube (A, B, C, D) can be created by folding the paper? There may be more than one right answer! Circle the correct ones.

Hint: Make the cube and check your answer!

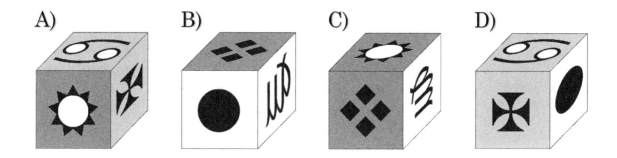

A)   B)   C)   D)

The pictures below have been cut up into different parts. Can you figure out what they are? Rearrange the pieces and draw the picture. Then, write down the name of the thing found in the picture.

1.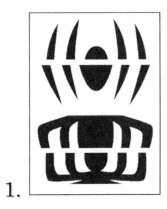

2.

3.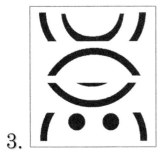

4.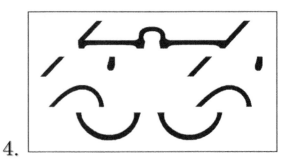

There are 3 words hidden behind the black shapes. Can you see them?

Hint: Draw lines around the black shapes to help you see better!

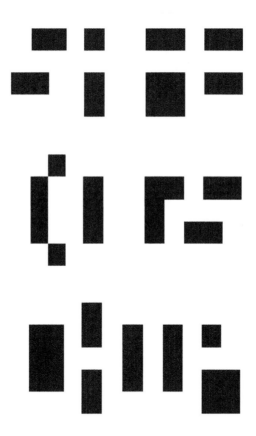

Visual Challenges

Addition ***** #46

Let's test your addition skills! Below are 6 numbers: 1, 2, 3, 5, 7, and 10. Pick any of the numbers and put them in the blank lines to create the correct equations. You can only use each number once for each equation, but you can use them again in another equation. We did one of them for you!

1 2 3 5 7 10

A) $1 + 2 = 3$

B) ____ + ____ = ____

C) ____ + ____ = ____

D) ____ + ____ = ____

E) ____ + ____ + ____ = ____

F) ____ + ____ + ____ = ____

Now that Johnny's clock is fixed, let's do some Math! Below are 2 patterns. Circle the correct answer for each.

Pattern #1:

A) 8:35   B) 8:40   C) 8:45   D) 8:50

Pattern #2:

A) 7:30   B) 6:45   C) 7:45   D) 6:30

Let's say that every letter in the alphabet weighs the same. Which word should be placed on the right side to balance the seesaw?

Hint: If consonants weigh 1 kilogram, then vowels must also weigh 1 kilogram! Count how much each word weighs, then add them up. The total on the left side of the seesaw must equal the total on the right side.

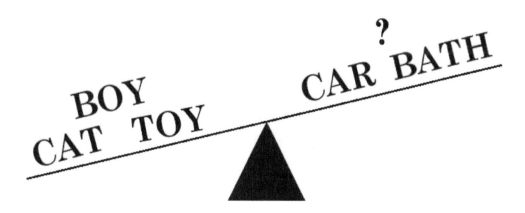

A) UP   B) DOWN   C) LEFT   D) RIGHT

Did you know that CAT + DOG = PETS? It makes total sense! Replace the letters with numbers from 0 to 9 so that the equation is correct.

Rules: You can only use each number once, and, both T's must be the same number!

$$
\begin{array}{r}
C\ A\ T \\
+\ D\ O\ G \\
\hline
P\ E\ T\ S
\end{array}
$$

Let's test your subtraction skills! Below are 6 numbers: 1, 2, 3, 5, 7, and 10. Pick any of the numbers and put them in the blank lines to create the correct equations. You can only use each number once for each equation, but you can use them again in another equation. We did one of them for you!

1 2 3 5 7 10

A) $10 - 3 = 7$

B) _____ – _____ = _____

C) _____ – _____ = _____

D) _____ – _____ = _____

E) _____ – _____ = _____

F) _____ – _____ = _____

G) _____ – _____ = _____

H) _____ – _____ = _____

Big Cube **✳✳✳   #51

Here's an easy question for you: How many small cubes do you need to make the big cube?

Hint: Draw each part and count!

Triangle Sum ***✳✳

The triangle below has three sides, and each side has three circles. Put the numbers 1 to 6 in each circle so that all sides add up to the same value.

Rule: You can only use each number once.

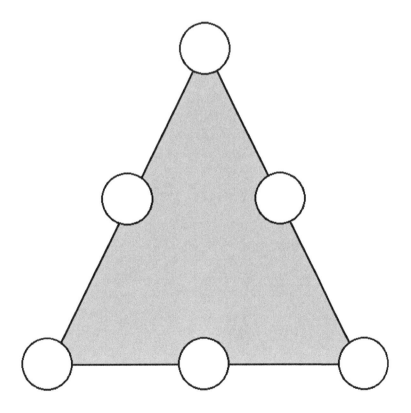

This And That ****** #53

Each of the questions below shows how much something is worth. For example in Question #1, a house is worth $300,000. You must complete the second part of each question by circling the correct number of items (houses, cars, or ribbons) on the right side of the arrows.

Question #1: = $300,000

$1,000,000 →

Question #2:

Question #3:

54   Math Problems

Let's test your multiplication skills! Below are 8 numbers: 1, 2, 2, 3, 4, 6, 8, and 12. Pick any of the numbers and put them in the blank lines to create the correct equations. You can only use each number once for each equation, but you can use them again in another equation. We did one of them for you!

1 2 2 3 4 6 8 12

A) 1 x 2 = 2

D) _____ x _____ = _____

B) _____ x _____ = _____

E) _____ x _____ = _____

C) _____ x _____ = _____

F) _____ x _____ = _____

Let's say that vowels in the alphabet weigh twice as much as consonants. Which word should be placed on the right side to balance the seesaw?

Hint: If consonants weigh 1 kilogram, then vowels must weigh 2 kilograms! Count how much each word weighs, then add them up. The total on the left side of the seesaw must equal the total on the right side.

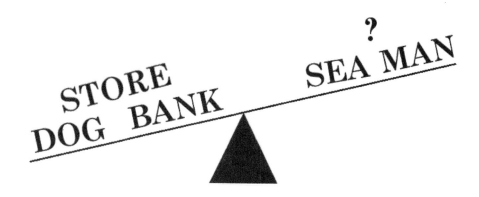

a) MONEY   b) CHIPS   c) STAR   d) GOOSE

Who knew that NORTH + SOUTH + EAST + WEST = EARTH? Replace the letters with numbers from 0 to 9 so that the equation is correct.

Rules: You can only use each number once. Remember, the same letters must be the same number!

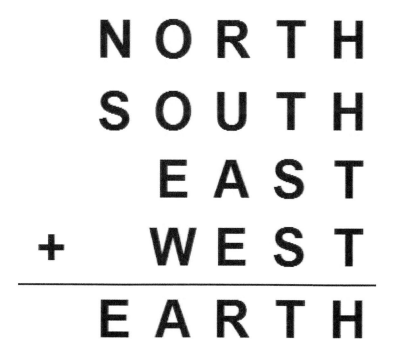

$$
\begin{array}{r}
N\ O\ R\ T\ H \\
S\ O\ U\ T\ H \\
E\ A\ S\ T \\
+\ W\ E\ S\ T \\
\hline
E\ A\ R\ T\ H
\end{array}
$$

Let's test your division skills! Below are 8 numbers: 1, 2, 3, 3, 5, 9, 10, and 15. Pick any of the numbers and put them in the blank lines to create the correct equations. You can only use each number once for each equation, but you can use them again in another equation. We did one of them for you!

1 2 3 3 5 9 10 15

A) $9 \div 3 = 3$

E) ＿＿＿ $\div$ ＿＿＿ $=$ ＿＿＿

B) ＿＿＿ $\div$ ＿＿＿ $=$ ＿＿＿

F) ＿＿＿ $\div$ ＿＿＿ $=$ ＿＿＿

C) ＿＿＿ $\div$ ＿＿＿ $=$ ＿＿＿

G) ＿＿＿ $\div$ ＿＿＿ $=$ ＿＿＿

D) ＿＿＿ $\div$ ＿＿＿ $=$ ＿＿＿

Missing Cubes ***** #58

Someone cut right through the large cube as shown in the picture below and removed entire rows of small cubes from left to right, front to back, and top to bottom.

How many small cubes are left over?

Hint: You must solve puzzle #51 Big Cube first!

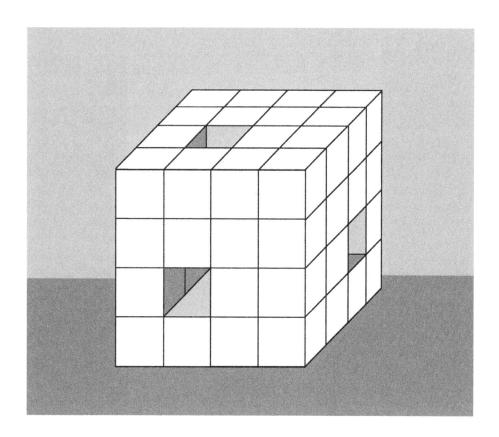

What It Takes ***✱✱   #59

Here are some questions to make you think.

Question #1:   If 1 🕷 can make 1 🕸 in 1 hour,

how many 🕷

does it take to make 4 🕸

in 2 hours?

Question #2:   If 2 🏃 can build 3 🏠 in 100 days,

how many 🏠

can 3 🏃 build

in 200 days?

Question #3:   If 5 👤 can catch 100 👳 in 1 year,

how many years does it take for

1 👤 to catch 60 👳 ?

The star below is made up of a pentagon and five triangles, and each triangle has three circles. Put the numbers 1 to 10 in each circle so that each triangle adds up to 19. One of the triangles is already done for you (9 + 4 + 6 = 19). Finish it!

Rule: You can only use each number once.

1 2 3 4 5 6 7 8 9 10

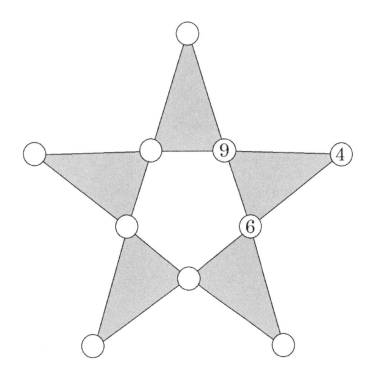

Math Problems

– Visual Puzzles –

Numbers Connect *☀☀☀☀   #61

Connect the matching numbers by drawing lines through
the grid. For example, 1 must connect to 1.

Rules: Lines can't cross each other, and only 1 line is
allowed in each tile (white square).

1.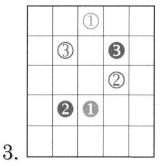

2.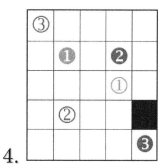

3.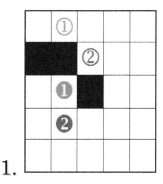

4.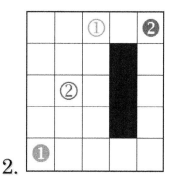

Draw the shapes below without lifting your pencil.

Rule: You're not allowed to backtrack.

1.

2.

3.

4.

It's Roboman again! Help him collect all the snowflakes and return to the white square. But be careful! The tiles fall when he moves off them.

Rule: Roboman can't step on a tile he's already visited.

Cut The Shapes ***** #64

There are 4 shapes below. For each shape, draw a continuous line (it doesn't have to be straight) to make two identical smaller shapes. The shapes can't be mirror images of each other!

For Shape #3, we've made a little cut for you already, and you must use it!

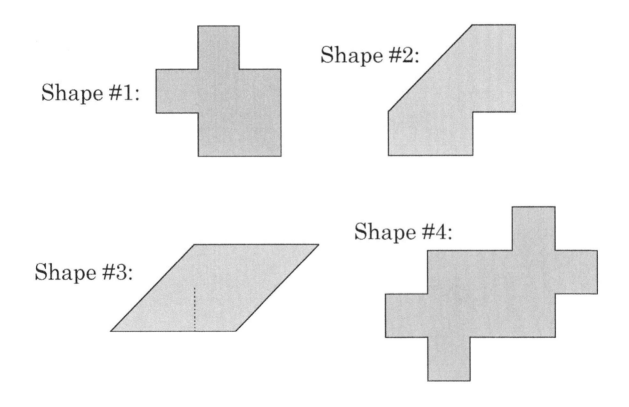

Shape #1:

Shape #2:

Shape #3:

Shape #4:

The pictures below are made up of "sticks." Can you figure out the solution? Draw your answer in the space provided.

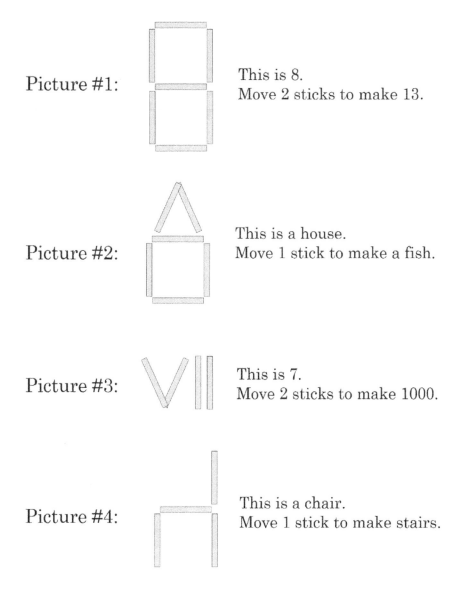

Picture #1:

This is 8.
Move 2 sticks to make 13.

Picture #2:

This is a house.
Move 1 stick to make a fish.

Picture #3:

This is 7.
Move 2 sticks to make 1000.

Picture #4:

This is a chair.
Move 1 stick to make stairs.

Use the small pieces in each puzzle to create the bigger shape (white grid of squares). Color the shapes in.

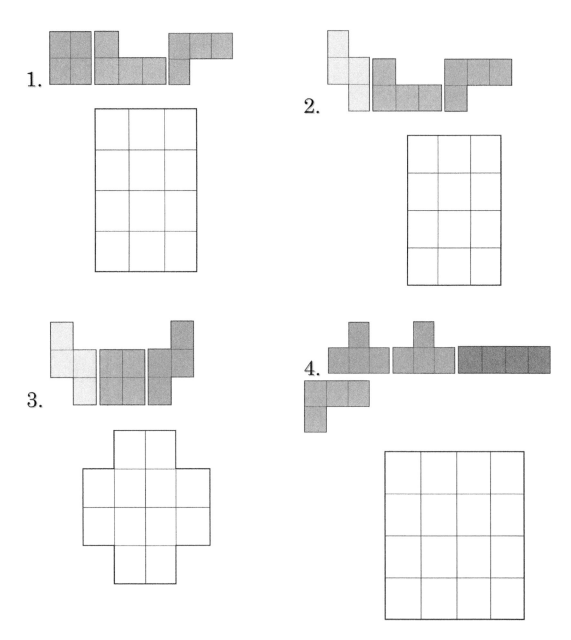

Picture Grid **✳✳✳ #67

The picture below shows a grid with two directions: left to right (x), and bottom to top (y). A coordinate (a point in the grid) can be written as (x, y), for example (5, 10). When you see this, find the number 5 in the x direction, and then go up to 10 in the y direction. Then, mark the spot with a dot. We've already done **Shape #1** for you! A dash between 2 (x, y) coordinates means you have to connect the dots. Connect them one after another to see the mystery shape!

Shape #1: (5, 10)-(3, 12)-(6, 13)-(8, 11)-(5, 10)
Shape #2: (13, 5)-(14, 12)-(19, 9)-(13, 5)
Shape #3: (4, 2)-(6, 8)-(8, 2)-(3, 6)-(9, 6)-(4, 2)

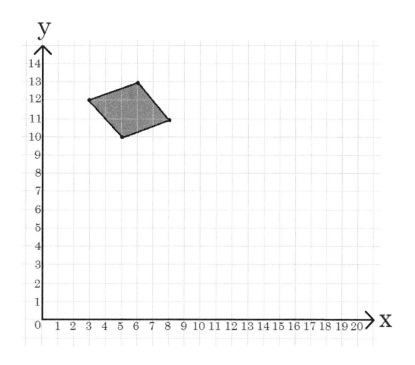

Cooking Show **✳✳✳   #68

What do you call a cooking show about fish?

Color in the all triangles to find out!

Numbers Connect 2 ***✱✱ #69

Connect the matching numbers by drawing lines through the grid. For example, 1 must connect to 1.

Rules: Lines can't cross each other, and only 1 line is allowed in each grid (white square).

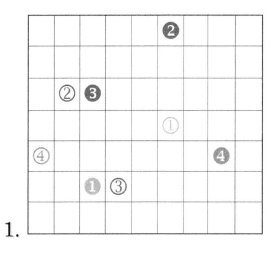

1.

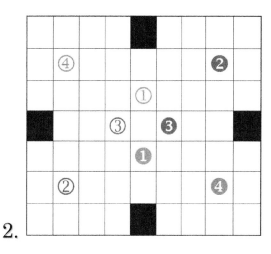

2.

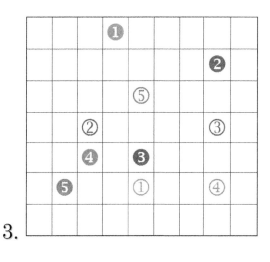

3.

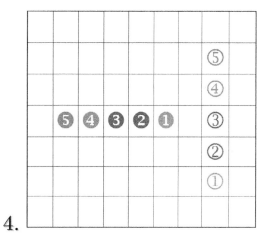

4.

Draw the shapes below without lifting your pencil.

Rule: You're not allowed to backtrack.

1.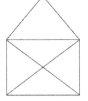

2.

3.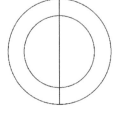

4.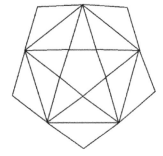

Falling Tiles 2 ***** #71

Help Roboman collect all the snowflakes and return to the white square. But be careful! The tiles fall when he moves off them.

Rule: Roboman can't step on a tile he's already visited.

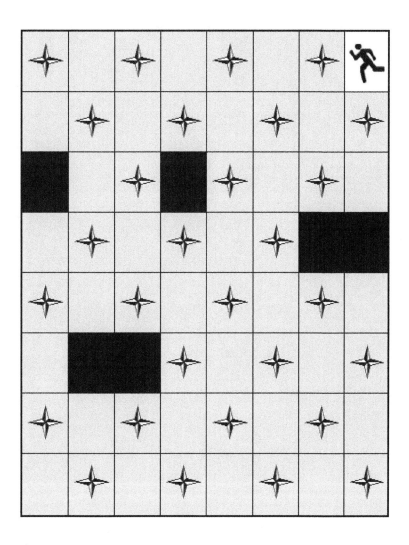

Stick Equations ***** #72

There are 6 equations below made up of "sticks." Equation #1 says 5 + 2 = 5, which is wrong. They all are! Your job is to fix them. For each equation, you must move only 1 stick to make it correct.

Equation #1: V + II = V

Equation #2: VI − V = III

Equation #3: IX + IV = XV

Equation #4: V − V = IX

Equation #5: X + X = I

Equation #6: IV − X = VI

Use the small pieces in each puzzle to create the bigger shape (white grid of squares). Color the shapes in.

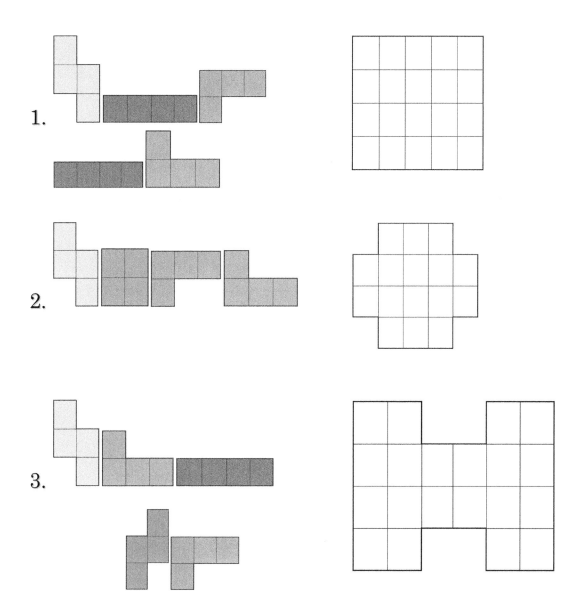

Separate the skulls from the snowflakes by creating a "fence" with 1 continuous line.

Rule: The line must start and end in the same spot.

There are 6 shapes hidden in the grid below. Connect all the coordinates to uncover the secret picture!

Shape #1: (4,2)-(2,4)-(2,6)-(4,8)-(6,8)-(8,6)-(8,4)-(6,2)-(4,2)
Shape #2: (14,2)-(12,4)-(12,6)-(14,8)-(16,8)-(18,6)-(18,4)-(16,2)-(14,2)
Shape #3: (5,5)-(7,9)-(13,9)-(9,5)-(5,5)
Shape #4: (9,5)-(6,11)
Shape #5: (15,5)-(12,11)-(14,11)
Shape #6: (6,10)-(5,11)-(6,12)-(8,12)-(9,11)-(8,10)-(6,10)

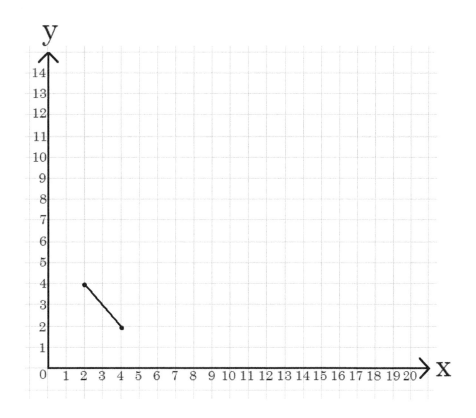

– Logic Puzzles –

Odd One Out *★★★★   #76

Which one of the four words below does not go with the others?

FORK
SPOON
SOUP
KNIFE

Random Letters **★★★   #77

Johnny's mother gave him a riddle. She wrote the following:

J F M A M J

What letter comes next?

Hint: Check your calendar!

Roboman receives a "bomb report" from the mayor, but it's incomplete. Each square is either a bomb or a number from 0 to 8. The number in a square tells Roboman how many bombs are around that square (up, down, left, right, and corners). For example, the square in the top left corner is 1, and there is 1 bomb around it (down diagonal right). Another example, the third square in the first row is 2, and there are 2 bombs around it (right, and down diagonal left).

Easy, right? Fill in the remaining 6 white squares with the correct numbers to complete the report.

1	1	2	💣	1	
2	💣	3		2	1
2	💣		2	💣	1
	2	💣	3		
0	1	3	💣	2	0
0	0	2	💣	2	0

Johnny thinks of a 3-digit number and asks his friend Sally to guess it. He gives her some hints:

* Each digit is either 1, 2, 3, or 4
* Each digit is different than the other (for example, the secret number can't be 223 because 2 is used twice)

To help Sally even more, Johnny promises to tell her how many digits she guessed correctly, but he doesn't tell her which spot ([1], [2], or [3]) is correct. Sally only has one guess left! Can you help her figure out the correct number?

Hint: Sally thinks the digit in spot [1] is 2, but is she right?

1 2 3 4

	[1]	[2]	[3]	
Guess #1:	1	2	3	0 Correct
Guess #2:	2	3	1	1 Correct
Guess #3:	3	1	4	1 Correct
Guess #4:	?	?	?	3 Correct

Letters In A Square *✱✱✱✱ #80

Fill in the blank squares with A, B, C, or D, so that:

* none of the letters appears more than once in each row and column
* none of the letters appears more than once within each section (gray or white area made up of 4 individual squares)

Here's one possible solution we found for you:

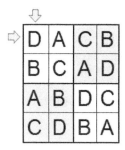

Now you try!

1.

2.

3.

Fill in the blank squares with numbers from 1 to 9 so that:

* none of the numbers appears more than once in each row and column
* none of the numbers appears more than once within each section (gray or white area made up of 9 individual squares)

	7			4	1		3	
3	6	4		9		8	5	1
	2	9	5	3	8	4	6	
7			8	5	9		2	6
6	8		1	2	7	5		4
9	5	2				7	1	
	9	6	2			1		3
2		7	3	8			4	5
8	3		9	1	4	6	7	

Sally's Picnic **✳✳✳   #82

Sally's having a picnic at the park and has invited four of her friends to join her. She's asked them to each bring an item to share. Sally brought sandwiches. Her friends James brought juice, Bob brought a blanket, and Candace brought cookies. The last friend brought a Frisbee. Can you figure out his name?

A) **Frank**   B) **Allen**   C) **Tom**   D) **Walter**

Three Honest Kids **✳✳✳   #83

Somebody in the family ate the last cookie in the jar, and dad's not happy! He goes to ask Jack, Jill, and John, and this is what they say:

Jack: *I didn't eat the cookie.*
Jill: *He didn't eat the cookie.*
John: *We didn't eat the cookie.*

If all three kids always tell the truth, and dad knows that one of them ate the cookie, which one did it? Explain.

Each question below is a riddle. The numbers in each equation tell you something about the shapes. Can you figure what they mean? Complete each question by writing down the correct numbers or letters for the question marks.

1.
□ ⬠ ⬡ = 4 5 6
✦ ▲ ◺ = 8 3 3
◇ ● ♥ = ? ? ?

2.
▲ ● ▯ = T C R
◺ ★ ♥ = T S H
⬠ ⬡ ■ = ? ? ?

3.
▲ ✦ ▯ = T E F
♥ ◺ ■ = T T F
★ ⬡ ⬠ = ? ? ?

Big Family ***** #85

The Smith family has 6 children. They were all born during springtime, and so their parents gave them the following names:

Sally

Peter

Rebecca

Ian

Nicolas

?

What's the name of the 6th child?

A) **Greg** B) **Tom** C) **Willy** D) **Mark**

Can you figure out the secret to these months and numbers? Draw a line from the month to the correct number. We did three of them for you.

Rule: Each number on the right side can only be used once.

JANUARY	3
FEBRUARY	4
MARCH	4
APRIL	5
MAY	5
JUNE	6
JULY	7
AUGUST	7
SEPTEMBER	8
OCTOBER	8
NOVEMBER	8
DECEMBER	9

Math Maze ***✳✳

Can you spell MATH? Your job is to go from START to FINISH by connecting each tile to the next tile around it (up, down, left, right, or corners) with a line.

Rules: You can only cross each tile once, and you are not allowed to skip tiles. Of course, you have to spell M A T H along the way. After H, you start over again with M!

START

M	H	T	M	M	A	T
T	A	A	A	T	H	H
H	M	H	M	H	T	M
A	T	T	A	M	A	A
H	T	A	H	M	H	T
M	M	A	M	H	M	A
A	H	T	A	T	M	T
T	H	M	H	T	A	H

FINISH

Roboman receives another "bomb report" from the mayor, but this time, it's missing both numbers and bombs! Each square is either a bomb or a number from 0 to 8. The number in a square tells Roboman how many bombs are around that square (up, down, left, right, and corners).

Fill in the remaining white squares with the correct numbers or a bomb.

Hint: Use the numbers to help you find all the bombs first.

1	1	1		2	
1				4	
1	1	2	💣		💣
1	2		2	2	1
💣	3		1	1	1
2			1		💣

Sally wants Johnny to guess her secret code made up of 4 tiles with pictures on them. She gives him some hints:

* Each tile is either GLASSES, AIRPLANE, BOMB, SNOWFLAKE, or HAND
* Each tile can only be used once

To help Johnny even more, Sally promises to tell him how many tiles he guessed correctly, but she doesn't tell him which spot ([1], [2], [3], or [4]) is correct. Johnny only has one guess left! Draw in the correct code for Guess #6.

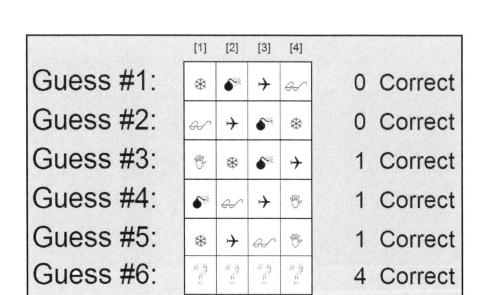

Fill in the blank squares with numbers from 1 to 9 so that:

* none of the numbers appears more than once in each row and column
* none of the numbers appears more than once within each section (gray or white area made up of 9 individual squares)

	9	4		5		8	3	
			8					9
8		3		9			5	
	4	1			8		6	7
				7	4	1	8	
6		7	9		3			
			2			3	7	
	6	2			1			5
5		8	7			6	1	

Logic Puzzles

The Butterfly **✳✳✳   #91

What do you call a butterfly that can no longer fly?

Hint: It's something you put on bread.

The Purple Friend *✳✳✳✳   #92

Have you met him before?

I'm big and purple, and will sing you a song
if you think I'm extinct, you're so, so wrong
I love to give hugs, and say I love you
won't you say you love me too?

Who is this loveable, purple friend?

Hint: He's from a kid's TV show.

River Crossing ***** #93

3 zookeepers and 3 monkeys arrive at a river which they must cross to get back to the zoo. There's a boat they can use, but it can only hold up to 2 of them at once. The monkeys are smart and can row the boat themselves without a zookeeper. However, they're very vicious! If there are more monkeys than zookeepers on any side of the river, the monkeys will attack the zookeepers. So, if there are 3 monkeys and 2 zookeepers on one side, the zookeepers are dead meat! How can the zookeepers plan their trip across the river so that they all arrive back at the zoo safely?

Weird Thanksgiving ***** #94

Tom celebrated Thanksgiving about a month before Sally. How is this possible?

Bless You ***** #95

You and your friend are talking and suddenly, he sneezes and says "bless you!" What do you say?

The Cheater **** #96

Johnny wants to play a game with his friends. He shows them 2 cards: a red ace, and a black ace. Then, he places them face down on a table and shuffles them around. To win, the friends must pick the red race. One person after another, they all end up picking the black ace. Sally's watching and realizes that Johnny's cheating. She notices that before placing the cards face down on the table, Johnny switches the red ace for a second black ace. So, no matter which card the friends pick, they always get the black ace.

It's Sally's turn to play! She's a nice girl and doesn't want to tell everyone that Johnny's a cheater. How can she play the game so that she still ends up winning?

Hint: Sally can say anything she wants during the game, but she can't call Johnny a cheater.

Sally's Family ***** #97

Sally's parents have five daughters:

Ava, Eve, Ivi, Ovo, and _____?

Half A Cup ***** #98

You're baking a cake and need to measure half a cup of sugar. You check the cupboards and find that you only have the following measuring cups: a 1 cup, and a 3-quarter cup. The cake recipe requires exactly half a cup of sugar. How can you accurately measure this amount?

Hint: You can pour the sugar from the cups back into a bag if needed.

Two Coins ***** #99

Johnny has 2 coins totaling 15 cents. One of them is not a dime, and the other one is not a nickel. How many dimes and nickels does Johnny have?

Jack's Family ***** #100

Jack is both the 3rd oldest and 3rd youngest child in his family. Assuming he has a mom and dad, how many people are there in his family?

Matching Marbles ****** #101

Jack has a bag filled with 5 red marbles, 5 green marbles, and 5 yellow marbles. Without looking, what is the fewest number of marbles he must pull out of the bag to guarantee that he gets at least two marbles of the same color?

Ladder Escape ****** #102

Roboman and three survivors must escape the headquarters of the evil Elector! They must climb up a long ladder through a dark, creepy tunnel filled with giant bugs that could eat them. The bugs don't like light and stay away from them when the tunnel's bright. Between Roboman and the survivors, they have one flashlight, and it only has 60 minutes of battery life remaining. **Roboman** is fast and needs only 4 minutes to climb the ladder, either up or down. **Survivor A** needs 8 minutes, **Survivor B** needs 20 minutes, and **Survivor C** needs 32 minutes. Also, the ladder is fragile and can only support two people at once.

How can Roboman and the survivors plan their trip through the tunnel so that they all make it out alive before the flashlight runs out of power?

Gummi Bears *✳✳✳✳   #103

You have 10 gummi bears and you eat all but 4. How many gummi bears do you have left?

The Butterfly 2 *****   #104

A riddle for lovers of words:

A butterfly has lost its wings
has lost its voice, it cannot sing
what's more, it's gained two big round eyes
give it a cross for the perfect disguise

The answer is a single word. What is it?

Hint: Solve "The Butterfly" riddle first.

The Three Sisters **** #105

Three sisters each have a Facebook account with lots of friends. They want to know the total number of friends they have, but there's a problem: they don't want to tell each other how many friends they have. How can the sisters find out the total number of friends and still keep secret exactly how many each has?

Rules: Their Facebook accounts are private, and they can't ask their parents or friends for help!

To help you get started, here's what each sister has:

Jessica — 137 friends
Jane — 99 friends
Julia — 114 friends

Hint: They'll need a pencil and paper!

Brain Teasers

– Answer Keys –

Mazes

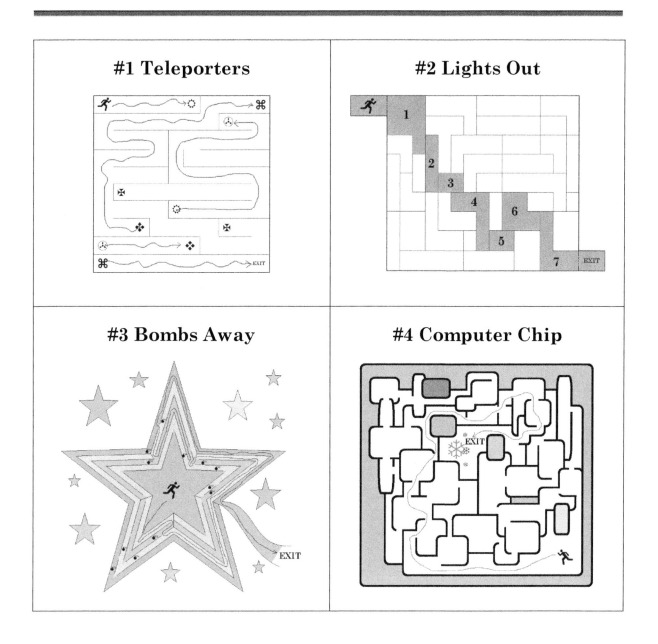

#1 Teleporters

#2 Lights Out

#3 Bombs Away

#4 Computer Chip

#5 Out Of Control

#7 Dizzy Dizzy

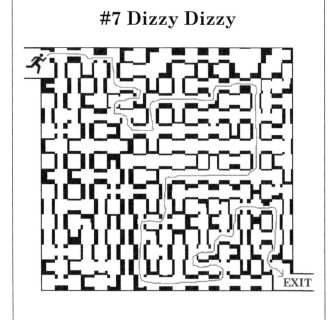

#6 Seeing Circles

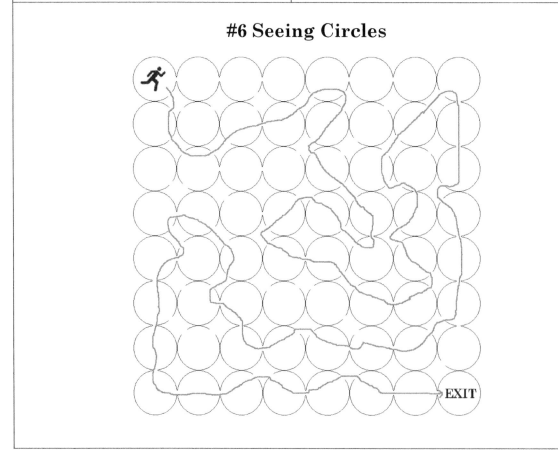

#8 Teleporters Galore

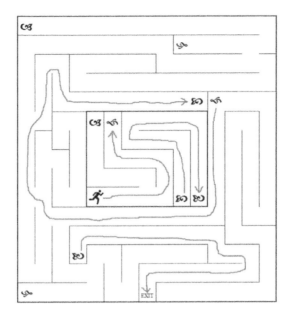

#9 Narrow Escape

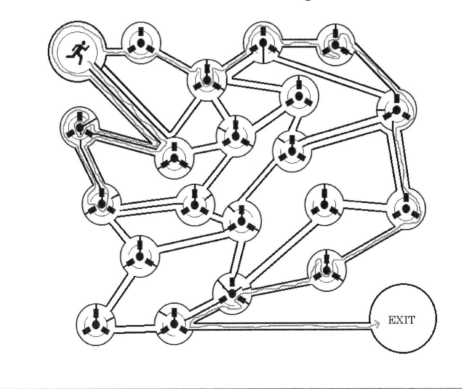

#10 Deadly Fall

#11 Funky Clouds

#12 Lights Out 2

#13 Out Of Control 2

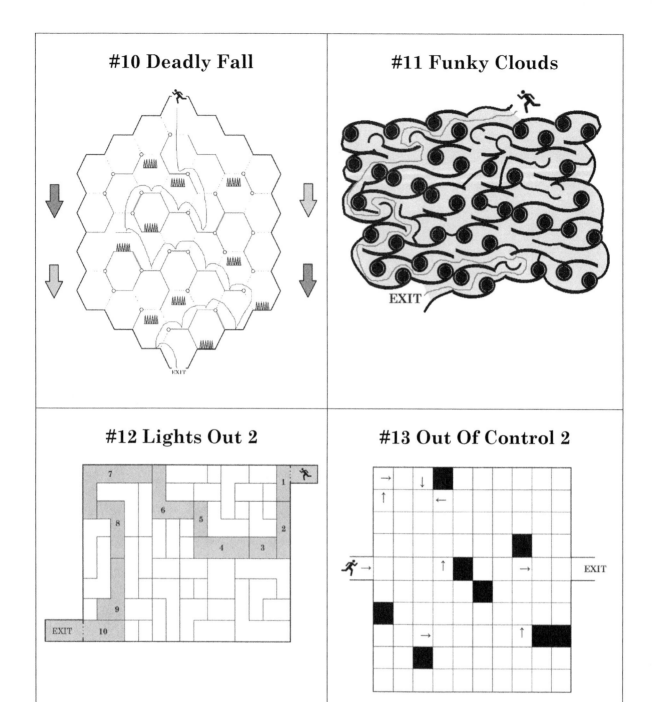

Answer Keys

#14 Triangles Of Doom

#15 Cup And Medal

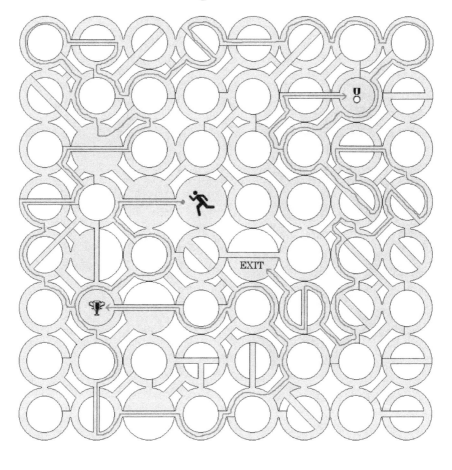

Word Games

#16 Word Square

	4	5	6
1	W	E	D
2	E	A	R
3	T	R	Y

#17 Secret Animals

1. BEAR
2. MONKEY
3. OWL
4. ZEBRA
5. LION
6. WHALE
7. BUTTERFLY
8. PENGUIN
9. CHIPMUNK
10. DEER
11. KANGAROO
12. OSTRICH
13. EAGLE
14. SEAL
15. IGUANA
16. GIRAFFE
17. RACCOON
18. SNAKE
19. BEAVER
20. RABBIT

What do you call two dogs that are very good friends? *Bro-collies*

#18 Easy Crossword

#19 Two Blanks

1. GODS
2. BODY
3. CODY
4. SODA

#21 Secret Riddle

Why wasn't the turkey at Thanksgiving dinner?

IT WAS ALREADY STUFFED!

#20 Animal Word Search

1. HORSE
2. PIG
3. COW
4. CAT
5. DOG
6. GOAT
7. SNAKE
8. OWL
9. RAT

#22 Word Square 2

#23 Missing Vowels

Sally's message is: *What are you doing right now?*

#24 Missing Consonants

Rob's message is: **I'm watching a movie.**

#25 School Subjects

1. HISTORY
2. MATH
3. GEOGRAPHY
4. ART
5. SCIENCE
6. MUSIC
7. LANGUAGES
8. PHYS-ED

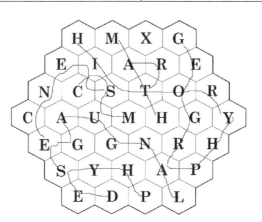

#26 Animated Films

1. FROZEN
2. ICE AGE
3. SHREK
4. FINDING NEMO
5. WALL-E
6. PINOCCHIO
7. THE INCREDIBLES
8. SLEEPING BEAUTY
9. UP
10. BEAUTY AND THE BEAST
11. MONSTERS INC
12. ALADDIN
13. TOY STORY
14. THE LION KING
15. KUNG FU PANDA
16. CARS
17. MADAGASCAR
18. RATATOUILLE
19. WRECK-IT RALPH
20. HOW TO TRAIN YOUR DRAGON

Where's an animal's favorite place to be? *Zootopia!*

#27 Three Blanks

1. SPRING
2. BORING
3. SPRINT
4. MARINA

#28 Hard Crossword

#29 Unscramble Me

What do you call two vegetables that are very good friends? *Bro-collis!*

#30 Sally's Secret Job

What is Sally's summer job?

SHE SELLS
SEASHELLS
BY THE
SEA SHORE.

Visual Challenges

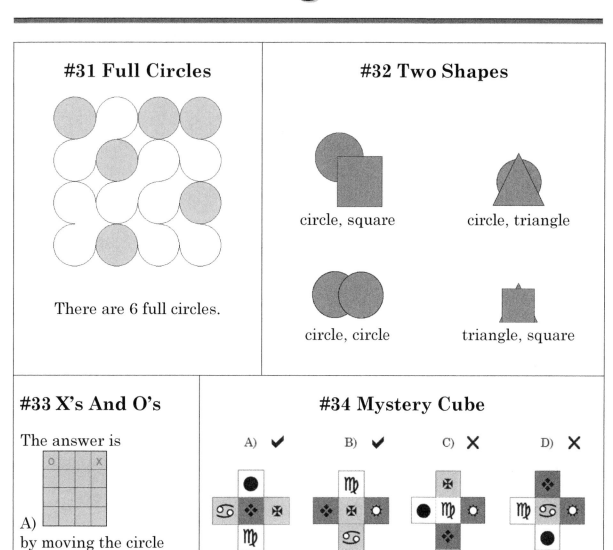

#31 Full Circles

There are 6 full circles.

#32 Two Shapes

circle, square

circle, triangle

circle, circle

triangle, square

#33 X's And O's

The answer is

A)

by moving the circle
LEFT 1 square, and the
X UP 1 square and
RIGHT 1 square.

#34 Mystery Cube

A) ✔   B) ✔   C) ✗   D) ✗

#35 Broken Clock

The clock is upside down! The answer is

D)

#36 Mixed Messages

Message #1:
THIS MESSAGE WILL SELF DESTRUCT IN FIVE MINUTES!

Message #2:
TEN, NINE, EIGHT, SEVEN, SIX, FIVE, FOUR, THREE, TWO, ONE, KABOOM!

Message #3:
ONCE UPON A TIME, THERE WAS A LITTLE BOY NAMED ALBERT WHO WANTED TO EAT CAKE ALL DAY. THE END!

Message #4:
ROSES ARE RED, VIOLETS ARE BLUE PUZZLES ARE SILLY, AND SO ARE YOU!

#37 Scrambled

ambulance

bicycle

airplane

police car

#38 True Symmetry

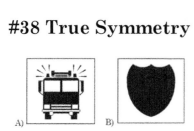
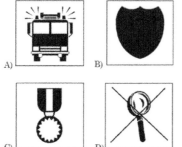

#39 Hidden Words

ART   GOD   PIE

#40 Tricky Triangles

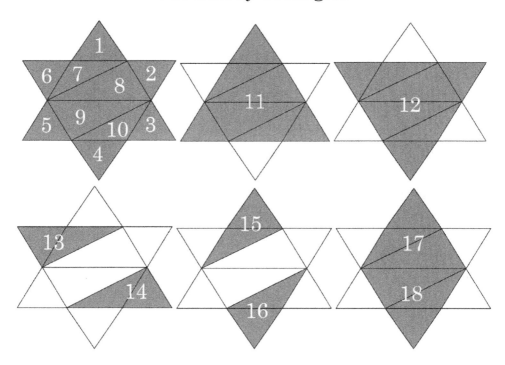

There are 18 different triangles in total.

#41 Three Shapes

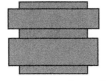

square, rectangle, rectangle

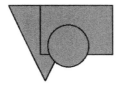

triangle, rectangle, circle

square, circle, circle

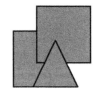

square, square, triangle

#42 Mystery Cube 2

The answer is

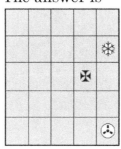

C)

by moving the cross sign UP 2 squares, the snowflake DOWN 1 square RIGHT 1 square, and the circle sign DOWN 1 square LEFT 1 square.

#43 Mystery Cube 2

A)   B)   C)   D)

#44 Scrambled 2

spider

ear

happy face

glasses

#45 Hidden Words 2

SAFE

DOGS

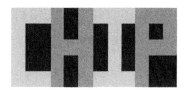

CHIP

Math Problems

#46 Addition

1. $1 + 2 = 3$
2. $2 + 3 = 5$
3. $2 + 5 = 7$
4. $3 + 7 = 10$
5. $1 + 2 + 7 = 10$
6. $2 + 3 + 5 = 10$

#47 New Time

The answer to Pattern #1 is C) by adding 25 minutes to the clock

The answer to the Pattern 2 is B) by subtracting 1 hour and 15 minutes to the clock.

#48 Word Seesaw

BOY = 3	CAR = 3
CAT = 3	BATH = 4
TOY = 3	UP = 2
9	9

#49 Adding Pets

Solution #1:
C = 8, A = 2, T = 9
D = 7, O = 6, G = 4
P = 1, E = 5, S = 3

$$
\begin{array}{r}
8\ 2\ 9 \\
+\ 7\ 6\ 4 \\
\hline
1\ 5\ 9\ 3
\end{array}
$$

Solution #2:
C = 9, A = 7, T = 8
D = 3, O = 0, G = 4
P = 1, E = 2, S = 4

$$
\begin{array}{r}
9\ 7\ 8 \\
+\ 3\ 0\ 6 \\
\hline
1\ 2\ 8\ 4
\end{array}
$$

#50 Subtraction

1. $10 - 7 = 3$
2. $10 - 3 = 7$
3. $7 - 5 = 2$
4. $7 - 2 = 5$
5. $5 - 3 = 2$
6. $5 - 2 = 3$
7. $3 - 2 = 1$
8. $3 - 1 = 2$

#51 Big Cube

The side of the cube facing us has 4 rows of 4 smaller cubes, which means 4 * 4 = 16 smaller cubes.
There are 4 groups of these rows, so we can use multiplication to get the total.

4 groups of 16 smaller cubes means 4 * 16 = 64 smaller cubes in total.

The answer is 64.

#52 Triangle Sum

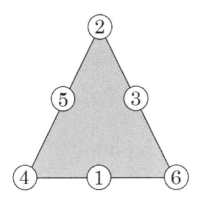

#55 Word Seesaw 2

STORE = 7	SEA = 5
BANK = 6	MAN = 4
DOG = 4	GOOSE = 8
17	17

#53 This And That

Question #1: 🏠 = $300,000

$1,000,000 →

Question #2: 🚓 =

→

Question #3:

#54 Multiplication

1. 1 x 2 = 2
2. 2 x 2 = 5
3. 2 x 3 = 6
4. 2 x 4 = 8
5. 2 x 6 = 12
6. 3 x 4 = 12

#56 Adding Directions

N = 3, O = 9, R = 6, T = 5, H = 0
S = 2, U = 4, E = 7, A = 8, W = 1

```
    3 9 6 5 0
    2 9 4 5 0
      7 8 2 5
+     1 7 2 5
─────────────
    7 8 6 5 0
```

#57 Division

1. $15 \div 5 = 3$
2. $15 \div 3 = 5$
3. $10 \div 5 = 2$
4. $10 \div 2 = 5$
5. $9 \div 3 = 3$
6. $3 \div 3 = 1$
7. $3 \div 1 = 3$

#58 Missing Cubes

The big cube has $4 * 4 * 4 = 64$ smaller cubes.
We remove 10 cubes from it (as shown in the picture below).

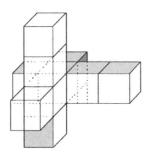

So, we are left with $64 - 10 = 54$ smaller cubes.

The answer is 54.

#59 What It Takes

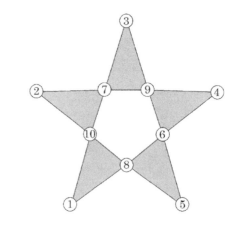

#60 Star Sum

Visual Puzzles

#61 Numbers Connect

#62 Continuous Lines

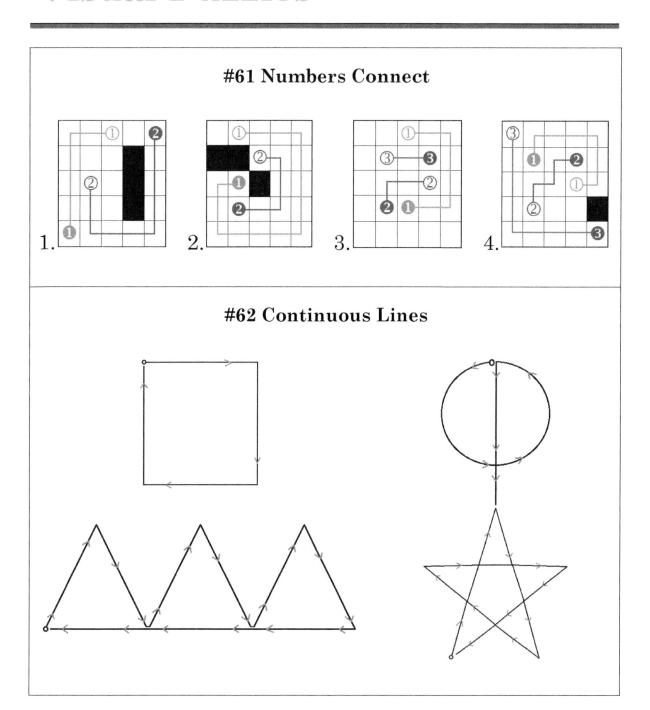

#63 Falling Tiles

#64 Cut The Shapes

#65 Tricky Sticks

#66 Puzzle Pieces

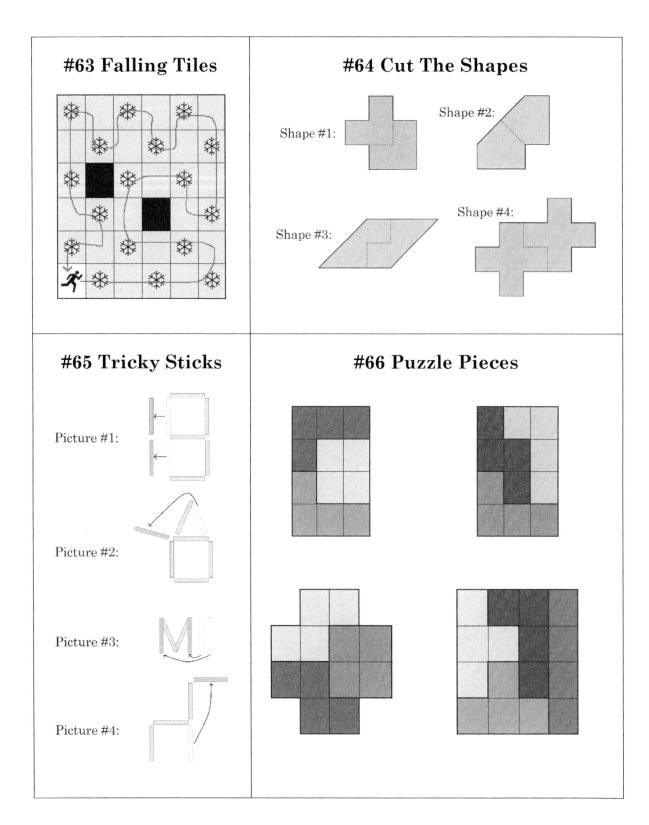

Shape #1:

Shape #2:

Shape #3:

Shape #4:

Picture #1:

Picture #2:

Picture #3:

Picture #4:

#67 Picture Grid

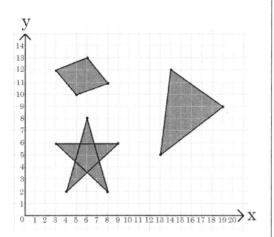

There's a diamond, a triangle, and a star!

#68 Cooking Show

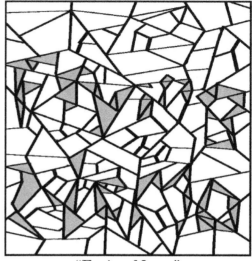

"Frying Nemo"

#69 Numbers Connect 2

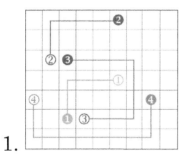

1.

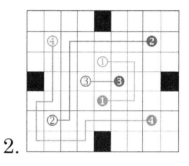

2.

3.

4.

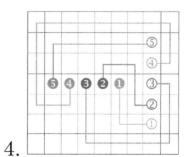

Answer Keys

119

#70 Continuous Lines 2

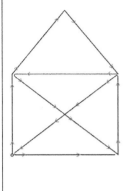 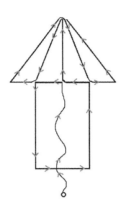 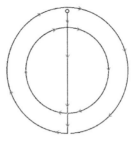 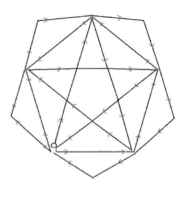

#71 Falling Tiles 2

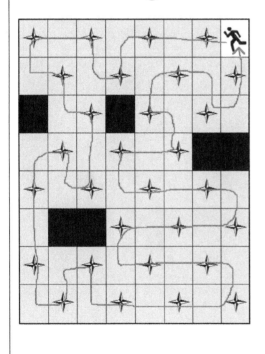

#72 Stick Equations

There may be more than one answer to each equation.

Equation #1:

Equation #2:

Equation #3:

Equation #4:

Equation #5:

Equation #6:

#73 Puzzle Pieces 2

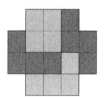

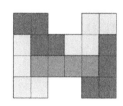

#74 Fence Off

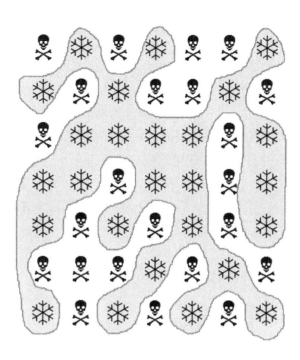

#75 Picture Grid 2

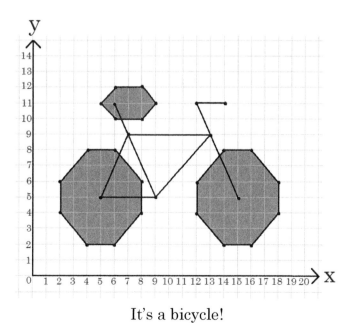

It's a bicycle!

Logic Puzzles

#76 Odd One Out

SOUP does not go with the other words. FORK, SPOON, and KNIFE are all kitchen utensils.

#77 Random Letters

They are the first letters of the month starting from January. J comes next.

January February March April May June July.

#78 Bomb Report

1	1	2	💣	1	0
2	💣	3	2	2	1
2	💣	3	2	💣	1
1	2	💣	3	2	1
0	1	3	💣	2	0
0	0	2	💣	2	0

#79 Johnny's Secret

	[1]	[2]	[3]	
Guess #1:	1	2	3	0 Correct
Guess #2:	2	3	1	1 Correct
Guess #3:	3	1	4	1 Correct
Guess #4:	3	4	1	3 Correct

Johnny's secret number is 3 4 1.

#80 Letters In A Square

A	B	C	D
C	D	A	B
D	C	B	A
B	A	D	C

C	B	D	A
A	D	B	C
D	A	C	B
B	C	A	D

B	A	D	C
D	C	A	B
A	B	C	D
C	D	B	A

#81 Sudoku

5	7	8	6	4	1	2	3	9
3	6	4	7	9	2	8	5	1
1	2	9	5	3	8	4	6	7
7	4	1	8	5	9	3	2	6
6	8	3	1	2	7	5	9	4
9	5	2	4	6	3	7	1	8
4	9	6	2	7	5	1	8	3
2	1	7	3	8	6	9	4	5
8	3	5	9	1	4	6	7	2

#82 Sally's Picnic

The last friend's name is Frank. Each friend brings an item that starts with the same letter as their name. James – juice, Bob – blanket, Candace – cookies, so Frank – Frisbee.

#83 Three Honest Kids

Jill ate the cookie. It's not Jack because he said so. When Jill said "He didn't eat the cookie," she was referring to Jack or John. John used the word "we", so he himself didn't eat the cookie as well. So the only possible answer is Jill.

#84 Shape Riddles

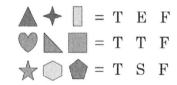

#85 Big Family

Greg is the name of the 6th child. If you take the first letter of each person's name, you get SPRING, which is when they were born!

#86 Count The Months

The number of letters in the month indicates what to connect to on the right.

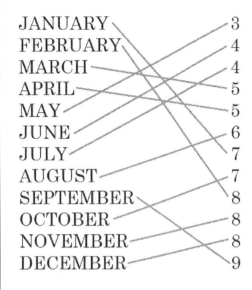

JANUARY	3
FEBRUARY	4
MARCH	4
APRIL	5
MAY	5
JUNE	6
JULY	7
AUGUST	7
SEPTEMBER	8
OCTOBER	8
NOVEMBER	8
DECEMBER	9

#87 Math Maze

START

FINISH

#88 Bomb Report 2

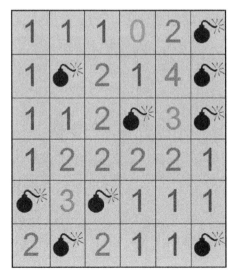

#89 Sally's Secret

	[1]	[2]	[3]	[4]	
Guess #1:	❄	💣	✈	👓	0 Correct
Guess #2:	👓	✈	💣	❄	0 Correct
Guess #3:	✋	❄	💣	✈	1 Correct
Guess #4:	💣	👓	✈	✋	1 Correct
Guess #5:	❄	✈	👓	✋	1 Correct
Guess #6:	💣	✋	👓	✈	4 Correct

Sally's secret arrangement is
BOMB, HAND, GLASSES, AIRPLANE

#90 Sudoku 2

2	9	4	1	5	7	8	3	6
1	5	6	8	3	2	7	4	9
8	7	3	4	9	6	2	5	1
3	4	1	5	2	8	9	6	7
9	2	5	6	7	4	1	8	3
6	8	7	9	1	3	5	2	4
4	1	9	2	6	5	3	7	8
7	6	2	3	8	1	4	9	5
5	3	8	7	4	9	6	1	2

Brain Teasers

#91 The Butterfly

A butterfly that can no longer fly is BUTTER. Cause it has no wings! Get it?

#92 The Purple

The answer is Barney.

#93 River Crossing

There are 3 zookeepers and 3 monkeys. Here's the plan to cross the river:

* 2 monkeys CROSS the river
* 1 monkey RETURNS
* 2 monkeys CROSS the river (at this point, all 3 monkeys have crossed)
* 1 monkey RETURNS
* 2 zookeepers CROSS the river
* 1 zookeeper and 1 monkey RETURN
* 2 zookeepers CROSS the river (at this point all 3 zookeepers have crossed)
* 1 monkey RETURNS
* 2 monkeys CROSS the river
* 1 monkey RETURNS
* 2 monkeys CROSS the river

All 3 zookeeper and monkeys have crossed the river!

#94 Weird Thanksgiving

Tom is from Canada, and Sally is from the United States. In Canada, people celebrate Thanksgiving in October, and in the United States, people celebrate it in November.

#95 Bless You

You ask him why he said "bless you" when he was the one who sneezed!

#96 The Cheater

There are 2 cards face down on the table and Sally must choose one. Sally can say she's picking the card on the left but turns over the card on the right instead. Because the card on the right is a black ace, she can say then that the card on the left must be a red ace, even though it's not flipped over and nobody can see it. Johnny wouldn't flip over the other card because it would show he cheated. Sally wins!

#97 Half A Cup

Here are the steps to get half a cup of sugar:
* fill the 3-quarter cup
* pour all the sugar from the 3-quarter cup into the 1 cup
* fill the 3-quarter cup again
* pour the sugar from 3-quarter cup into the 1 cup until the 1 cup is full
You are now left with half a cup of sugar!

#98 Sally's Family

Ava, Eve, Ivi, Ovo, and Sally.

#99 Two Coins

Johnny has 1 dime and 1 nickel. "One of them" is not a dime, and the "other one" is not a nickel.

#100 Jack's Family

Jack is the middle child of 5 children in his family. Including his mom and dad, there are 7 people.

#101 Matching Marbles

Jack needs to pull out at least 4 marbles. The first three can all be different colors (red, green, or yellow), but the 4th marble must be a match.

#102 Ladder Escape

Here's the plan:
* Roboman and Survivor A CLIMB (8 minutes have elapsed)
* Roboman RETURNS (8 + 4 = 12 minutes have elapsed)
* Survivor B and Survivor C CLIMB (12 + 32 = 44 minutes have elapsed)
* Survivor A RETURNS (44 + 8 = 52 minutes have elapsed)
* Roboman and Survivor A CLIMB (52 + 8 = 60 minutes have elapsed)

#103 Gummi Bears

You have 4 gummi bears left because you eat all of them "but" 4.

#104 The Butterfly 2

The answer is: BOOT

A butterfly has lost its wings
(it can't fly, so it becomes BUTTER)
has lost its voice, it cannot sing
(can't sing means we remove UTTER and are left with B)
what's more, it's gained two big round eyes
("big round eyes" refer to the letters OO, so we get BOO)
give it a cross for the perfect disguise
(a "cross" refers to the letter T, so we get BOOT)

#105 The Three Sisters

Jessica has 137 friends, Jane has 99, and Julia has 114.
In order to keep these numbers a secret, Jessica decides to add a secret number that only she knows to her number of friends. Let's say this secret number is 50.
So, 137 + 50 = 187
She writes this new number down on a piece of paper and then passes it to Jane (without showing Julia). Jane adds her number of friends to this number.
So, 187 + 99 = 286
She writes this new number down on a piece of paper and then passes it to Julia (without showing Jessica). Julia adds her number of friends to this number.
So, 286 + 114 = 400
She writes this new number down on a piece of paper and then passes it to Jessica. Jessica then subtracts the secret number from the total.
So, 400 − 50 = 350

This means, the sisters have a total of 350 friends!

About The Author

J.J. Wiggins worked in the IT industry where he enjoyed a long and fruitful, yet tedious career. He has since retired and now spends his days with his family, doing his darndest to make them laugh.

http://amazon.com/author/jjwiggins

Other Works

Printed in Great Britain
by Amazon